T O

_____

F R O M

_____

D A T E

_____

THE GREATEST GIFT

A CHRISTMAS STORY

BY MELODY CARLSON

ILLUSTRATED BY JACK STOCKMAN

GOLD 'N' HONEY BOOKS · SISTERS, OREGON

THE GREATEST GIFT
published by Gold 'n' Honey Books
a division of Multnomah Publishers, Inc.

© 1997 by Melody Carlson
Illustrations © 1997 by Jack Stockman

Design by D² DesignWorks

International Standard Book Number: 1-57673-190-1

Printed in the United States of America

For information:
Multnomah Publishers, Inc.
Post Office Box 1720
Sisters, Oregon 97759

LIBRARY OF CONGRESS CATALOGING-IN-PUBLICATION DATA

Carlson, Melody
The greatest gift / by Melody Carlson : illustrated by Jack Stockman.
                        p. cm.
Summary: Grace, the smallest of the angels, chooses to leave the glory of heaven to become
the Christmas star that lights the Son's way to earth.
ISBN 1-57673-190-1 (alk. paper)
[1. Angels—Fiction. 2. Christmas—Fiction. 3. Stars—Fiction. 4. Christian life—Fiction.]
I. Stockman, Jack, 1951-   ill. II. Title.
PZ7.C216637Gr 1997
[Fic]—dc21   97-19582
                                              CIP
                                              AC

98 99 00 01 02 03 - 10 9 8 7 6 5 4 3 2

FOR MOM -M.C.

FOR KARA KATHRYN VEJR -J.S.

Christmas is a time of wonder — a time of miracles. It's a time to pause and reflect, and perhaps be swept away, once again, by the awe of a moment that changed the world forever. We all have heard many Christmas stories over the years; some are told from a historical perspective, others with flourish and flair. We invite you now to enter into a fanciful story that celebrates the true spirit of Christmas.

Of course, the events in this story never happened quite like this, but if you allow the child in you to listen, a miracle could happen in your heart. And it will happen again and again — each time you give and receive the greatest gift.

All of heaven rumbled with excitement. The very air seemed charged with energy and joy. The Big Event was coming soon, and there was so much to be done. Some angels polished their wings until they glistened and shone. Some tuned their celestial instruments to play notes that had never been heard. Others practiced beautiful new songs. All to celebrate the Big Event!

Little Grace, the smallest of the angels, sat with her wings folded and looked upon these activities with dismay. "I don't see why He has to go down there," she whispered to her angel friend, Joy.

"Oh, Grace," explained Joy, "it's all part of the Father's big plan. The Father dearly loves His people on earth, and it's the only way to save them."

"But why? Why must He send the Son? I love the Son so much. I will miss Him greatly." A diamond tear slid down Grace's nose.

"I know, little one, but it will all be for the best. You'll see. The Son must deliver a special message from the Father. It will be a very happy day indeed!"

"Attention! Attention!" called Gabriel. All the angels stopped their preparations and turned to listen, for they knew that Gabriel was a very important angel. "I need an angel to perform a very special mission," said Gabriel. "It has to do with the Big Event." The angels crowded around. Eager to hear more, they chattered with excitement and began to ask questions. It seemed everyone wanted to volunteer. But Grace stood behind the other angels. All she could see were the backs of fluffy white angel wings.

"Quiet, quiet!" called Gabriel. "Let me explain. The Father needs one of you to volunteer to be a star."

"A star?" echoed Magna, a very handsome angel. "I would love to be a star—"

"Please," interrupted Gabriel. "Let me explain all the facts before anyone volunteers. It is not an easy mission. The Father needs someone brave and strong to be this star. An ordinary star will never do. The Father wants an angel who will understand this mission—"

"Judah is very wise," said one angel. "He understands many things."

Gabriel held up his hands. "Please listen. There is more. All volunteers need to know that whoever accepts this mission will no longer be an angel."

Gasps of surprise were heard throughout the heavens. The angels' eyes grew wide as they stared at Gabriel in wonder. They whispered to each other. How could it be true? What was happening?

"No longer an angel?" asked Joy in a trembling voice from the back row.

"That is right," said Gabriel.

"But why?" asked Magna.

"All I know is that this star is very important. Not an ordinary star," said Gabriel. "The Father wants this star to light the way for the Son's entrance to earth. And this star will be the very first from heaven to greet the Son. Now, do I have any volunteers?"

For a brief moment, the heavens grew still. Not a single angel spoke. No one volunteered. Grace thought about the Son going to earth all by Himself, and another diamond tear slid down her nose. She brushed it off and shyly stepped forward.

"I will go," said Grace in a quiet voice. She was unable to look up into the mighty Gabriel's eyes.

All the angels turned, and Grace stared down at her tiny feet. What if Gabriel thought she was too little? He had said that the Father needed an angel who was strong and brave. She was neither.

"Are you absolutely certain, Grace?" asked Gabriel.

She looked up at him and nodded. "Yes, I would like to be a star for the Son."

"It won't be easy," said Gabriel. "Did you fully understand what I said about not being an angel anymore?"

Grace nodded again and swallowed hard.

"Then so be it," said Gabriel, and he gave her a smile that warmed her heart. "Come, and I will explain what you must do."

Grace followed, trying not to hear the hushed voices of the angels behind her.

"Is Grace giving up being an angel?"

"Does she know what she's getting into?"

"God go with you!" called Joy.

Grace turned and waved.

Gabriel instructed Grace about her mission. It was really quite simple. She was to fly down to a village called Bethlehem and position herself above an inn on the outskirts of town. Gabriel told her that when the time came, she would know what to do next.

"Remember, Grace," said Gabriel just as she was ready to leave, "God is with you always — even until the end of time."

Grace nodded. "Thank you. I will remember. Good-bye, Gabriel." Then she turned her face toward earth and began to fly.

Grace had always enjoyed flying. She was a good flyer — lighter than air and faster than light! Her friend Joy had often complimented Grace on her flying skills.

Soon she reached the place where heaven's light met earth's darkness, and the air became cold and sharp as a knife. The wind howled in the night, beating against her wings with fierce fury, but still she continued toward earth.

Clouds of blackness wrapped around her with icy fingers, but still she continued toward earth. She had never felt so alone or so cold. But one special thought kept her warm. The Son was also coming to earth — and she would be there to welcome Him!

Finally, just as Grace felt she couldn't travel another minute, she spotted the little town called

Bethlehem. And just as Gabriel had described, there was the inn right on the edge of town.

Grace sighed as she settled into place directly above the inn. She was weary and cold and

slightly homesick — she had never been away from heaven before. But she waited in the sky.

And when she saw the sun peek above the horizon, she felt a small surge of hope.

But as the sun fully lit the sky, she saw how tattered her wings had become, and her gown

was now torn and shabby. Worst of all, she didn't look anything like a star! How could this

be? Had she made this long, hard journey only to be a scruffy little angel hanging in the sky?

Several diamond tears slid down her nose, but she remained in place, waiting.

The sun rose higher and higher, and Grace felt a small seed of warmth begin to glow in the center of her like a red-hot coal. But it wasn't a bad feeling. After a while, it flowed from her chest and into her arms and her legs and her wings — until it finally exploded with little pops and tingles out of her fingers and toes and feather tips!

As the sun began to slip into the west, Grace felt this heat radiate from her body. And when day turned to night, Grace could see she was being transformed. She was changing from an angel into a star!

It was a wonderful feeling of warmth and cheer and light.

But as the sky grew darker, she looked about the heavens in dismay. There were millions and millions of other stars all around! Many of them seemed bigger and brighter than she. Had she forgotten something? Had she done something wrong?

She liked being a star, but wasn't she supposed to be a very special star — the biggest and brightest star ever? Wasn't she supposed to show people on earth that the Son had finally come?

Thoughts of the Son's upcoming arrival kindled an even greater warmth, and suddenly she began to glow more brightly than ever. Then flashes of heat began to explode inside her. Before long, she had become the biggest, brightest star in the entire sky. The biggest and brightest star ever!

Grace's brilliant light washed over the dark surface of the earth, making it almost as bright as day. From her place in the sky she could see the figures of two travelers entering the little town below her. It must be Mary and Joseph! Everyone in heaven knew that these two had been chosen to take care of the Son when He arrived on earth.

To her surprise, they stopped at a different inn. Oh no, had she gotten it wrong? But instead of going inside, they went back out to the street. They went from inn to inn to inn. Grace giggled to herself. Mary and Joseph must not know which inn they were supposed to stop at.

Grace shot out special beams of light to Mary and Joseph, hoping they would notice that she was above the right inn. At last, they stopped at the inn below her. But then a strange thing happened. The innkeeper led them not inside the inn, but to the back of the inn. And there, he showed them to the place where animals were kept. Why, it was nothing more than a stable!

Grace blinked in amazement. Did the Father realize that His Son was going to enter earth in a place where donkeys and cows were kept?

Grace knew that the big moment was coming. The Son would soon be here! She waited,

shining brightly in the darkness.

Then finally, in the middle of the night, the sounds of a crying baby drifted upward like

sweet music. And Grace knew that it had happened! She looked down upon the little stable,

and there He was. At long last, the Son had arrived!

More bursts of heat exploded inside her. Pure beams of starlight poured down to the sta-

ble like water from a glittering fountain. Would the Son know that the star above Him was

really Grace, a gift sent from His Father? Could He understand that this was heaven's way of

welcoming Him to earth? And did He know how much she loved Him?

Grace twinkled and sparkled as if to say, "Hello, down there! This is Grace up here!" Oh, how she loved being a star for Him!

Then she heard the familiar sounds of joyful angels singing and loud shouts of glory. On the nearby hillside, she saw all the angels of heaven gathered in a huge celebration. The Big Event was happening all over now!

She watched in delight as her friends announced the birth of the Son to a group of shepherds on the hill. A small part of her longed to join them in the singing and fun. But then she looked down at the Son below her, sleeping sweetly in the manger, and she knew there was no place in heaven or on earth that she would rather be!

Soon the shepherds streamed over the hills and rushed toward the sleeping town of Bethlehem. Grace stretched her bright rays as if to point to the stable and tell them, "See, here He is! Here is the Prince of heaven!"

She watched happily as, one by one, the shepherds fell to their knees and worshiped the Son. Her heart filled with fresh fire as she saw them welcome Him, and she burned more brightly than ever.

For the next few days, Grace stayed in the sky above the stable. She continued to glow brilliantly for all to see. And many, seeing her starlight, came to worship the Son. She worshiped Him, too. She watched as Mary and Joseph cared for Him, still amazed that the Son of the Most High had come to earth as a helpless baby. Then she thought about how she had given up being an angel to come to earth as a star. Still, being a star seemed much more glorious than being a baby.

One day, Mary and Joseph began to pack their things to leave the little stable. Grace watched as Joseph helped Mary onto the donkey, then gently placed the Son in her arms.

Where were they going? Where were they taking the Son?

Grace watched sadly as the little family left Bethlehem and traveled south. She watched them until they became a tiny speck in the distance and then finally disappeared altogether.

Oh, if only she were an angel. Then she would spread her silky wings and follow the Son wherever He went! But alas, she could not move. She sighed as she stared at the empty stable below. Diamond tears sizzled and sputtered as they met the heat of her fiery star beams.

Suddenly, she felt very alone.

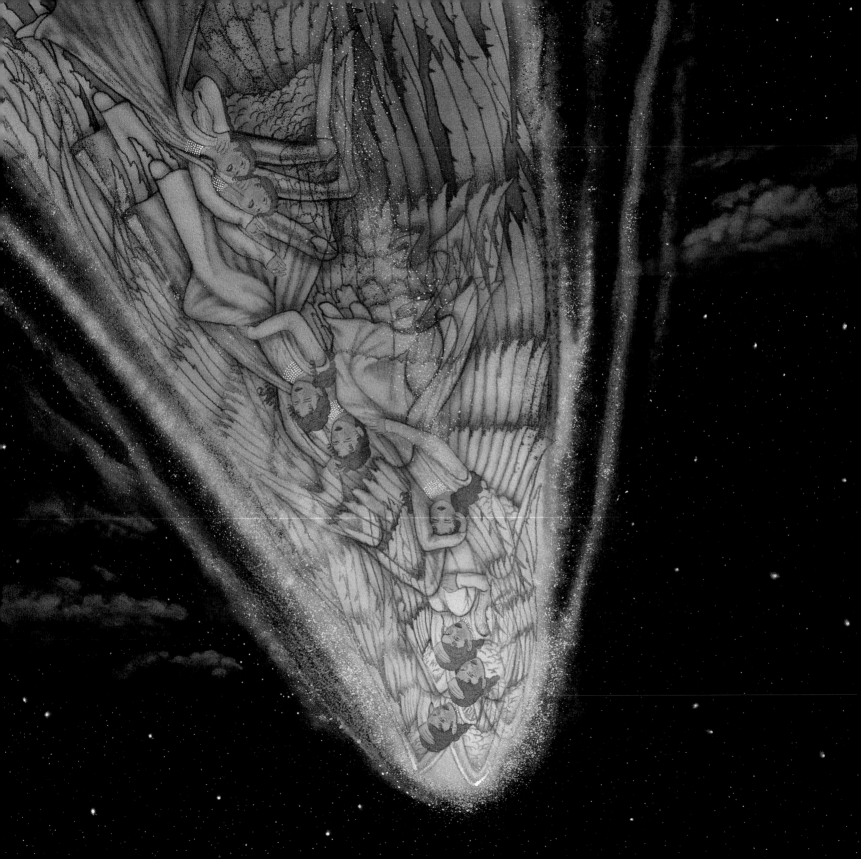

As the sun set, Grace realized that her own starlight was fading fast. Try as she might, she couldn't stir up a spark or a glimmer.

And when the night came, she barely glowed at all. She grew colder by the minute — and very, very lonely. The Son was gone now. Grace had no need to twinkle and blink, no need to try to make Him smile.

Now, more than ever, she longed to return to heaven — to be an angel again. But she remembered what Gabriel had said. Once she became a star, she could no longer be an angel. What would become of her now?

Suddenly she felt herself begin to slip. She was falling from the sky! She had never felt like this before. She had always been lighter than air and able to fly faster than light. But now she was tumbling uncontrollably to earth.

Falling was the most horrible thing, and she tried desperately to catch herself, but all she could manage was to make herself spin. Fortunately for the town below, her spinning propelled her north of Bethlehem. But all the same, she plummeted down, down, down — faster and faster!

God is with me, God is with me — even to the end of time, she told herself as she hurled

toward the ground below. Finally, she landed with a mighty boom that shook the earth. And

there she lay, unable to move.

It was very dark and very cold — and very, very lonely.

When at last the sun came up, she could see that she had landed on a hillside. And she

could see what she had become.

No longer an angel. No longer a star. Now Grace was simply a huge, ugly stone, the same

color as the darkened sky just before dawn.

And there she lay, day after day, week after week, month after month.

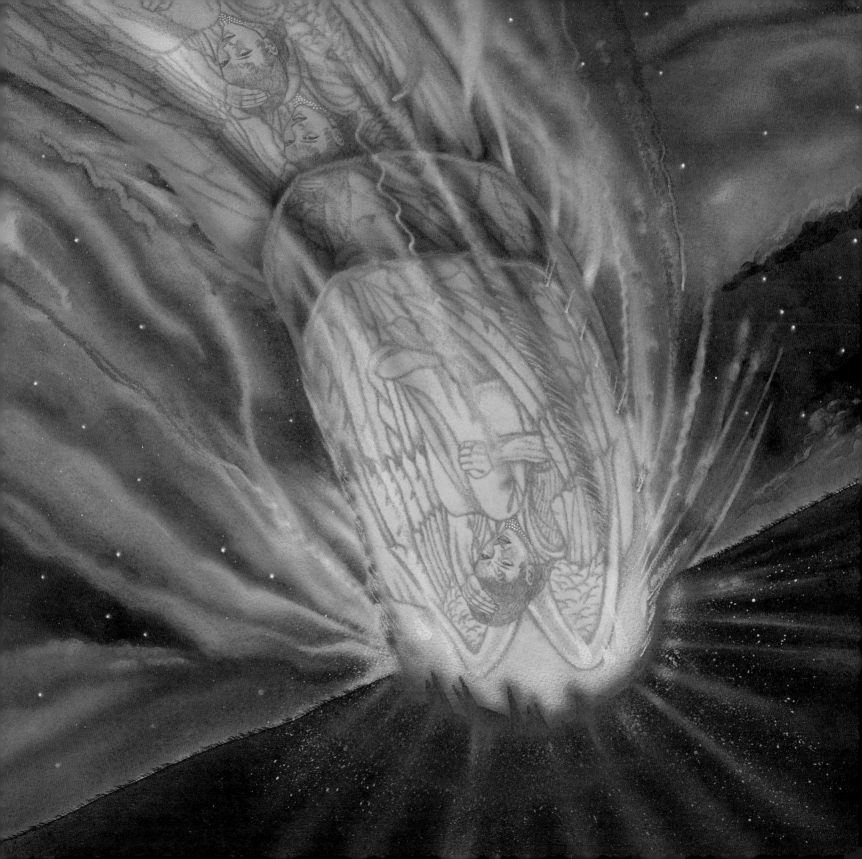

Grace knew this must be what the Father wanted for her, and she tried to take pleasure in the birds and the trees around her, and the flowers that came in the spring. But it was a lonely life. She missed her angel friends and she missed the freedom of flying. But more than anything, she missed the Son.

Year followed year, and there she lay — cold and alone. Sometimes she wondered if the Son was still on earth. Or had He finished His mission and returned to heaven? And sometimes she wondered if the Father had forgotten her altogether.

One spring evening just before the sun went down, Grace heard strange voices. They sounded very sad. What could be wrong? Why were they crying? As they came closer, she could see they were carrying a man. She watched as they laid the man in a cave next to her. Then to her surprise, they rolled her over to block the entrance, and then they left. She gazed at the person in the cave, and suddenly — she knew.

That was the Son lying there. And the Son was dead!

But how could it be? Why would the Father allow this?

In silent grief she watched over Him. A deep pain felt as though it would split her cold stone body into many, many pieces. But for His sake, she would hold on. She would watch over Him forever.

Strange men stood outside the cave. She did not know why. She did not even care. All she cared about was the Son.

Then on the morning of the third day, a startling thing happened. Grace heard joyful voices. To her amazement, her angel friends had come. Even her friend Joy was with them.

At last! The Father had sent help!

The next thing Grace knew, they were rolling her away from the cave. She realized that they didn't even recognize her. How she longed to cry out, "It's me, Grace! I'm watching over the Son!" But alas, she was only a stone and could not speak.

And then the most wonderful thing happened. The Son came back to life!

He stood. He walked. He talked. And Grace had never, in her entire life, felt so very, very glad. The Father had not forgotten His Son after all! Surely this was all part of the great plan — the plan to save the people on earth.

As quickly as they had come, the angels left, eagerly chattering about the great work they still must do. Oh, how Grace longed to join them! But they did not know she was there. Because, of course, she was only a stone.

And what could a stone do?

Suddenly Grace felt a surge of warmth upon her cold stone surface. It was warmer than the summer sun. Warmer than the golden streets of heaven. Even as a star, Grace had never felt such radiant warmth. And then she saw Him standing before her in all His glory!

"Arise, little one," He said in a gentle voice. "You did not think I would leave you behind?"

Instantly, Grace felt the heavy weight of the cold, hard stone crumble away. She was free! Once again she was lighter than air. And she was clothed in a shimmering white gown, with angel wings that sparkled like starlight. She bowed before Him, whispering, "Thank you!"

"Thank you, Grace," said the Son. "You have given the greatest gift. You willingly laid down your life for another. And I shall take you back to heaven, back to the Father."

Although Grace was no longer a stone, she was so excited that she could neither speak nor move. And although Grace was no longer a star, she was so full of joy that she shone with bright light.

There was great rejoicing in heaven when the Son returned. But the most joyous, the most jubilant, the most thankful angel of all — was Grace!